Kristy's
Winter Cutting Garden
A WATERCOLORING BOOK

Contents

Schiffer Publishing Ltd

4880 Lower Valley Road • Atglen, PA 19310

DEDICATION

To my Lord and Savior, for teaching me the meaning of true Joy.
To my husband, Adam, for never wanting me to be someone I'm not.
To Isaac, for showing me a whole new life.
To Mama T, you inspire me every day.
To Mom and Dad, for loving, pushing, and understanding me.
And to Unkie, who taught me to keep my nose to the grindstone.

ACKNOWLEDGMENTS

This book is the result of heartfelt collaboration. Without the insight and smarts of so many whom I hold dear, this series of watercoloring books would not be possible.

To the young illustrators whose passions and talents contributed to many pages of this book: Rachel Behm and Madison Smolsky, your skills astound me again and again.

To Amy, my best friend and kindred spirit, who instilled in me the confidence to write in the first place.

To #themomentals, who give me the space and time to make these crazy dreams come true.

To Kelley, for helping me write when the nights were long and the words were short.

To Katie, for her meticulous attention to all artwork seen on these pages.

To Steph, for jumping in and making it happen!

To Kristen, for being the best proofreader around.

To Jillian, for always lending an ear and being brutally honest.

To Elizabeth Hardin, for her stunning calligraphy.

"And perhaps I will stay with you, or even spend the winter,
so that you may send me on my way wherever I may go."

1 Corinthians 16:6

White Amaryllis

One Christmas season when I was about thirteen, I painted a red amaryllis in a simple pot. I loved that painting, even though I wanted to paint a white amaryllis and didn't know how. My parents framed the masterpiece and eventually it was donated for auction, but it has never been far from my mind.

Painting tip: Painting bold but clean reds can be a challenge. Mixing equal parts water and pigment for the first washes will give you a bright, clean base. Once dry, layer more color onto the page (about seventy percent pigment, thirty percent water).

On being an artist: Artists ask what if, what else, what's next? These questions are difficult to answer, but integral to fostering a creative life. Never accept status quo; question everything.

Snowy Winter Scene

Here, deer peek around pine trees covered in fresh snow. Other forest creatures make shy appearances here and there. If I were to walk the fifty feet or so from my backyard to the woods, this would likely be my view.

Painting tip: Don't be afraid to use color in the snow, shadows, and reflections with a wet-in-wet technique. Sheer color (made with tons of water) with a light touch of the brush is the best way to capture the look of snow.

On being an artist: Artists seek relaxation. I'm no stranger to working hard or even burnout, but over the years I've learned to recognize when I need a respite from the everyday chaos. Listen to your instincts and take a break.

Evergreen Composition

As a teenager, I remember that the old pine trees around our house felt absolutely ancient and magical. They provided shade and a secret hideaway no matter what the season. In winter, however, my best friend and I would collect fresh boughs to decorate the house. Sap was everywhere, of course, but the strongest memory is the smell of fresh pine.

Painting tip: Drybrush and texture are your friends on this page. Using the side of your brush, and more pigment than water, are key. Scratch the brush around to create interest within branches. Using a small brush, add thin strokes of color side by side to add loft to the evergreen boughs.

On being an artist: Artists don't need to know all the answers. We may want them but recognize that attempting to figure it all out, all at once, will get us nowhere in our art making! Instead, we need to believe in our abilities, if only for ten minutes—just enough time to get some brushstrokes down on the page.

"In a world where many desperately seek to know all the answers, it is not very popular to believe . . . ."
—*Maya Angelou*

Winter Berries

In the winter, scavenging a few branches with the little fruits still holding on can be tricky, but the effort is worth it.

Painting tip: Vary the value of color— from light pink to deep, dark scarlet. Value refers to the lightness or darkness of a color. Black, for example, is the darkest value, while white is the lightest value.

On being an artist: Artists have the power to make beauty. I've always felt incredibly lucky to be a painter. We have a desire to make things better and more beautiful. Even if our work never leaves the house or is never posted on Instagram, it can make life a bit better.

"Our primary defaults are exhaustion and guilt. Meanwhile, we have beautiful lives begging to be really lived, really enjoyed, really applauded."
—*Jen Hatmaker*

CROWNED FOX

Well, who doesn't want to paint a pretty fox with a flower crown? But seriously, this sweet little critter is just begging for juicy watercolor brushstrokes and maybe even a touch of shimmer ink!

Painting tip: Fan brushes are a luxury, but you can pick one up fairly affordably. Stiff bristles, about an inch long, fan out from the barrel. Use the fan brush to create cool dry-brush effects. The fox's fur is the perfect spot to try it out!

On being an artist: Artists persevere. My uncle, who I called Unkie, loved the phrase "keep your nose to the grindstone." Keep working, keep living, keep loving what you do. I hear you, Unkie.

OWL ON A BRANCH

Owls have a moody charm we all seem to love. Don't forget to paint the background in some wonderful way. You'll see suggestions on the front pages of this book.

Painting tip: Cerulean blue is the perfect choice for skies. Use a large brush (at least a #10 round) and a lot of water to keep the pigment moving until you have filled the entire space.

On being an artist: Artists are patient. Author Brenda Ueland, who wrote about creativity, believed our imagination often works slowly and quietly. I'm all about the quiet, but slowly? Really? Regardless, know this—patience and trust in yourself will catapult your efforts farther than you can fathom.

PINECONE VARIETIES

Pinecones remind me of snowflakes. Each one is completely different.

Painting tip: Adding white to the pinecone tips could be a lovely way to create depth and texture. Any brush will work, but the dagger style (see suggested materials) will give you the ability to create a thin-to-thick stroke easily. White brushstrokes will especially pop on a background of darker greens.

On being an artist: Artists are okay being uncomfortable. Painting is always teetering on the edge of discomfort. Even as a professional painter, I feel a certain uneasiness when I sit down to a blank page. Knowing where to first touch the page always feels like I'm about to jump off the high dive—scary, but soon to be exhilarating!

"You can choose courage or you can choose comfort, but you cannot have both."
—Brené Brown

WINTER BOUQUET

Amaryllis resemble the daylilies of summer, and they are so magical because they adore blooming in winter. Appearing in shades of red, white, coral, burgundy, fuchsia, and practically everything in between, these elegant blooms will never disappoint.

Painting tip: Create one color out of two with the ombre technique. Lay down a good amount of water on the page. Add a touch of one color to the wet page and let it go. Add a touch of a second color away from the first. Using a clean brush, move the color around a bit with light dabs here and there.

On being an artist: Artists have courage. You do, I know you do! Search for your artistic courage every single day. Paint with your eyes closed, paint without bending your elbow, paint with the brush in your mouth. I know these suggestions sound strange, but they will force you to loosen up and ignore the typical way of painting, and put you on the path to finding your courage.

"Do you have the courage to bring forth this work? The treasures inside you are hoping you will say yes."
—Elizabeth Gilbert

WINTER SCENE

In early winter as a child, when I'd leave the house for school, I often saw a family of deer just outside our door. The mama deer would come so close, much to the buck's dismay, and the experience felt like a gift every time it happened.

Painting tip: The spatter technique is fun for winter paintings, especially when you choose shimmer or white spatter over darker watercolor you've painted. Sheer versions of blue and lavender spatter also work well to accent snowy areas.

On being an artist: Artists envision. We seem to know what our day will look like even before it begins to unfold, right? It is so easy to fall into a predictable routine and assume we can't fit in time to paint. Envision what your day could be by allowing a bit of time for painting. It's nice, isn't it?

STAR OF BETHLEHEM

Star of Bethlehem are curious blooms. Their tons of texture and long life are their best qualities. When in bloom, star of Bethlehem vary from green bud to popping pods and then sculptural petals with tiny black centers.

Painting tip: Using dirty color to add last-minute details is an exciting way to bring out the drama of your painting quickly. Using a blend of all colors on your palette (yup, you heard me correctly), load a #1 or #2 round brush with the mixture, blot lightly, and begin to add touches with very little pressure. The centers of flowers, small crevices between petals, and even a bit of edging around the leaves will benefit from this technique.

On being an artist: Artists collect books. I've always wanted a library in my home. Something about seeking out obscure and unwanted books energizes me. Reference books can spark ideas better than any glance at a screen. Holding a book in your hands turns the creative process into something tangible.

POINSETTIAS AND CARDINAL

My uncle spent his career at a local nursery. Always figuring out the best fertilizer to make plants grow huge and building machinery to automate the planting process, he was quite the genius. Each Christmas, he would deliver a truckload of poinsettias to our home. It was a magical time.

Painting tip: Consider tearing the page out to work. For best results, you'll need to tape the page down on the edges. To ensure easy removal when complete, stick the tape to your skin to remove some of the stickiness before applying.

On being an artist: Artists pull artistry into their daily lives. Infusing artistry into all aspects of your life is easier than you might think. Imagine enjoying a cup of tea in a hand-painted heirloom teacup, or mixing your family's famous cookie recipe in a hand carved wooden bowl. Taking advantage of small moments to celebrate small treasures puts you on the path to living artfully.

"There is an art to living that is far above the base human instinct of survival . . . ."
—*Jennie Allen*

HOLLYBERRY WREATH

The first artwork I created in colored pencil was a hollyberry wreath. Falling in love with the intricate berries, stems, and leaves was easy.

Painting tip: When covering a large area with watercolor, keeping a wet edge is important. A wet edge is a section of color that stays wet as you work to fill a page. If the edges start to dry, you won't be able to blend the colors and a harsh edge will result. So work steadily and with focus, and you'll have a lovely, smooth effect across the entire surface.

On being an artist: Artists see first. Long before I knew how to articulate my painting process, I knew exactly how my eyes seemed to just connect with a flower or landscape while painting. I could see details others didn't; I could use color to sculpt a convincing hillside, but words escaped me. Get comfortable with seeing. Get comfortable with silence.

"Seeing comes before words."
—*John Berger*

Winter Berry Variety

Southern arrowwood, northern bayberry, and hollyberry are the main berry-producing shrubs indigeneous to Pennsylvania. Each has its own personality and flair. Here, I've documented a tangle of berries just begging to be painted.

Painting tip: Red isn't the only color to consider when painting this page. Try indigo, violet, shades of green, and even gold to mix things up. If you're looking to capture a strong winter vibe, opt for less vibrant hues.

On being an artist: Artists avoid distractions. You can't do good work when your attention is pulled in many directions. When you're sitting down to paint for just a small chunk of time, you deserve to enjoy that time uninterrupted. So put the phone away, unless you're listening to music.

Hellebores in a Teapot

Hellebores start blooming just after snowdrops. What an amazing follow-up! Here, the hellebores, also called Lenten roses, are tucked inside a vintage silver teapot.

Painting tip: Painting a surface that looks like shiny silver is a challenge, but simpler than you might imagine. Mix a variety of gray and gray/blue pigments on your palette. Most will be quite light (using a lot of water), a few will be medium tone (a fifty-fifty ratio of water to pigment) and one or two will be darker (very little water). Add these colors in strategic areas to create the elongated rectangles and curves seen in the silver's reflection.

On being an artist: Artists can paint like children. Children dive into their art, oblivious to possible failure and frustration. Expression pours from their soul with no pretense. As artists, we learn to see through our fears and feed our abilities.

Snowdrops

Snowdrops are the growing season's first flower to appear, and in Victorian times they represented hope—how appropriate, right? Small and unassuming, the little white bell-shaped blooms possess tremendous strength and fervor. I adore the thought that a flower can be strong in personality but delicate in appearance.

Painting tip: This page is a great place to apply thick layers of white acrylic. Use mindful brushstrokes, avoiding the urge to over brush one area. Use varying pressure as you lay down strokes to reveal thick and thin areas of paint. Layer a piece of wax paper over your dry page while the acrylic cures.

On being an artist: Artists are particular. After years of painting, I've learned the benefits of having a strong and consistent setup. I need a particular type of water container, number of paper towels, favorite brushes, and type of light for my painting session to go smoothly. I can paint amidst utter chaos, but my ideal setup is always waiting for me.

"They insist on good tools, and they develop a
remarkable order in their preparation for work."
—Robert Henri

Winter Wreath

Something about hanging a wreath on the door says winter. Every year, I gather up at least five wreaths from around our home and studio, and once they are hung, I instantly feel warm and cozy and ready for the season. Pinecones, pine boughs, holly leaves, and berries make up this full, textural wreath.

Painting tip: When painting a detail-laden piece like this, colors can get heavy and muddy quickly. Don't be afraid to use the white of the paper when applying brushstrokes. Ignore the urge to perfectly fill in each leaf, berry, or sprig. Leave some spontaneous unpainted moments throughout the page to maintain a light and airy feel.

On being an artist: The painting journey on which you're about to embark on isn't an easy one, but it is definitely one of the most rewarding. In times of frustration, you may wonder if you'd learn quicker with expensive classes or if you lived in an artsy town, but let me be the first to say this: you have everything you need right in this moment to succeed.

"Your geography and your biography do not determine your destiny."
—Simon T. Bailey

Christmas Cactus

My parents have an epic Christmas cactus that has been passed down for generations. About three feet wide and four feet tall, this plant needs a lot of space and love, and even though it chooses to bloom at Easter instead of Christmas, it is cherished just the same.

Painting tip: Most leaves have a bit of a sheen. Leaves look most alive and healthy with a bit of a shine here and there. To create the look, simply leave a bit of white on your leaf or mix a bit of white with green to paint highlights.

On being an artist: Artists paint with their children. Hashtag artistmeetsmother is a powerful Instagram account documenting painters continuing their artistic life into motherhood. Integrating children into your artistic endeavors is a solid way to stay creatively active and inspired.

Snowflakes

As a kid, I would attempt to capture snowflakes to make out their one-of-a-kind, intricate patterns. Of course I was never successful, remaining baffled as to how such intricate patterns could reside inside such tiny flakes of snow.

Painting tip: Get wild: use unexpected color or add pattern inside each snowflake. Using a pencil, sketch patterns in small areas or in the background to detail and interest.

On being an artist: Artists work in the imaginary. There are times when a little bit of nonsense is the best remedy for a creative block. Sit down to the page, get out the paints, and just make a bit of crazy. Use colors that don't make sense and refuse to care about the end result. Just have a blast!

Amaryllis Bulbs

The mark of a classic botanical illustration is the appearance of not only flowers in the composition, but also bulbs. Some of the world's most famous botanical illustrators, such as the Bauer Brothers, Rory McEwen, and Jean Louis Prevost, documented the stages of growth from seed or bulb to full blossom.

Painting tip: This page would be amazing if you used gold inks and a fine brush to add curious details throughout the finished piece. Depending on the ink you choose (see materials and recommendations), you may want to water it down a bit. Even easier: use a fine-tip gold pen.

On being an artist: Artists balance. Botanical artists are known for creating incredibly life-like impressions in paint, but attempting to copy this style as a beginner could be frustrating. Instead, balance your efforts between painting what you see (more realistically) and painting with emotion and instinct.

"I paint not the things I see but the feelings they arouse in me."
—Franz Kline

Snowy Mountain Scene

Behind my childhood home was an expanse of land complete with a picturesque pond. In winter, my family would venture out to ice skate, or what I call "ice walk." Regardless of our skating prowess, we had a blast and made fun memories.

Painting tip: Paint a scene by moving around the page and not working in one area for too long. This will help the scene to feel cohesive, with the same level of detail everywhere.

On being an artist: Artists thrive in community. You may not be painting to become famous or make money, but just the same, you need a bit of comaraderie. Working alone, always, can squelch your vision and diffuse your momentum. Working alone, without conversation about art, will only satisfy for so long.

"No one—not rock stars, not professional athletes, not software billionaires, and not even geniuses—ever makes it alone."
—Malcolm Gladwell

FIELD OF PINE TREES

After all the flowers fade away and the leaves fall from the trees, we are left with the beauty of evergreens. The landscapes I call home are filled with the greenery of these giant pines.

Painting tip: Mix a huge variety of greens to keep a simple scene interesting. Experiment by making at least fifty versions of green. The act of mixing this many shades will broaden your color palette horizons.

On being an artist: Artists make it happen. Creative souls seem to find a way, regardless of skill, roadblocks, and half-starts, to see their art come to fruition. Know that because you're here, reading this, you have the same drive and desire.

DEER FAMILY

Deer live on our property, and in the early morning fog they startle as our doors open. In the evening, as we pull into the dark driveway, their golden eyes flash from our yard.

Painting tip: Consider your focal point. Add the most detail to the part of the painting where you want the viewer's eye to linger.

On being an artist: Artists know the creative value in taking a walk. Getting out in the breeze and noticing the curious shapes the light makes filtering through the pines is unlike any other motivation to paint.

"In every walk with nature one receives far more than he seeks."
—John Muir

CHIPMUNKS

These spunky little critters are fun to watch from my back porch. I love how they play with each other, rolling, running, tumbling, and jumping to their heart's content.

Painting tip: Experiment with watercolor brands. At the back of this book I've suggested numerous paint brands. As your love of watercolor grows, try out the more saturated pigments that professional-series watercolors offer. You'll be amazed by their color and vibrancy.

On being an artist: Artists know how to be careless. Allowing yourself to make mayhem on the page, with no care for rules or order, will allow your heart, mind, and spirit to meet and make friends.

MOOSE, ELK, EAGLE, DEER, BUNNIES

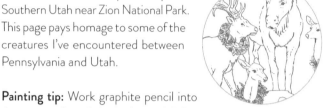

About a third of our year is spent in Southern Utah near Zion National Park. This page pays homage to some of the creatures I've encountered between Pennsylvania and Utah.

Painting tip: Work graphite pencil into damp paper for subtle shading and definition. When the pencil tip hits wet pigment, the graphite slowly takes on the color of the pigment. Experiment on scrap paper first.

On being an artist: Artists start now. I've been there: buried in work when a good idea strikes. If you're like me, midnight comes and the idea just won't relent and it's spilling from your brush onto the page. Artists just start . . . now.

"Don't think about making art, just get it done..."
—Andy Warhol

MISTLETOE AND POMANDERS

One year after Christmas, my hubby and I forgot to include the mistletoe in the boxes of decorations headed for the attic. We have yet to take it down, and our mistletoe gets a lot of off-season use now!

Painting tip: Consider adding a fourth pomander behind the other three. Use a light touch with a pencil so that you can erase mistakes.

On being an artist: Artists see the beauty each day holds. Even after a night of little sleep, I can wake up feeling joyful because the prospect of painting for even five minutes at some point during the day puts me in a good state of mind, and I am grateful.

"Life itself is the most wonderful fairytale of all."
—Hans Christian Andersen